SALLY FRETWELL'S

THE POWER OF
COLOR

www.sallyfretwell.com

For more information please contact Sally Fretwell
toll free at (888)830-1860
email to sally@sallyfretwell.com
or visit www.SallyFretwell.com

Library of Congress Cataloguing-In-Publication Data
    Fretwell, Sally

        Interior Design, Interior Decorating, Architectural Consulting, Home
        Building, Home Remodeling, Use of Colors

            1. Interior Design 2. Interior Decorating 3. Architectural
            Consulting 4. Home Remodeling 5. Architectural Psychology
            6. Fengshui

    ISBN: 0-9721548-4-1

    Sally Fretwell. -- 1st Edition

Printed in Canada

Editing: Syd Farrar
Graphics and photo editing: John C G Thompson
Cover Design: Jen Fleisher (www.CharmedWorks.com)
Page Design and Layout: C Pierce Salguero (www.salgueronet.net/books)

Acknowledgements

Color makes the world go round, it is everywhere, for us to enjoy. I can not thank, John Thompson, a wonderful photographer, enough for his help with this book. His computer design skills, patience, appreciation and understanding of color, love of Nature and technical knowledge enabled him to create what I saw in my mind's eye. He gave me colors to choose from and like a kid in a candy store, colors to play and decorate with. I thank Syd Farrar for expanding, arranging and editing all my ideas, thoughts and words so that I was able to say in print what I truly wanted to express to the reader. He understood that everyone sees things in their own way and tried to make sure that everyone gets a little something out of the book.

Preface

My intention in this book, The Power of Color, is not to choose colors for you. My ultimate goal is to give you ideas and examples of a broad range of colors pulled from interesting color palettes. I want to show how you can surround yourself with colors from your most favorite places in the world. These colors are your favorites for their own special reasons. That is the power of color.

How colors play together ultimately makes all the difference in the mood you are able to create when you "color your world." I want to intrigue, inspire, entice, and even prod you to try new things. When I look at some of the beautiful colors pictured in the following pages, it is not only how the colors enhance each other, but perhaps more importantly, it is the interplay between them that intrigues and excites me.

I have included several pictures of the canals of Venice. You have the faded stucco buildings, the colorful flower boxes and awnings, the reflection of the homes in the canal water, the color and fluidity of the canal and the movement of the gondolas on the water. Each element and color of the picture can be taken and examined both individually and as a whole to see how they work together to form a beautiful picture and setting. Such should be the case when you are designing how you are going to put together a room. Take your individual elements such as your wall color, furniture fabric, flooring or window treatment and have them work together as a whole to create a living space you love to be in.

The Impressionist painters of the 19th century had a style of painting that was characterized by visible brush strokes, light and vibrant colors and ordinary subject matter. In their paintings, they explored how the presence or absence of light affected a painted scene. The Impressionist painter, Georges Seurat, in his paintings of the French countryside often would use the tiniest dots of color from the tip of his paintbrush, which when combined and viewed in its totality produced beautifully painted landscapes.

With all due respect to Seurat, I have used a widely available computer photo imaging program called Photoshop, to identify colors in a photograph. Using the program, I can place my pointer on a specific part of a picture and the software program can generate the exact color that I am pointing to. Often this color, as exampled on the pages of this book, is quite different from the color that we think we see in the picture. This is because the color that we see is made up of a multitude of different shades, variations and tones that come together to form an impression of color that we see with our mind's eye.

The point here is that while I have, in this book, isolated and drawn out "dots" of color that make up the color that you see, it is also something that you can do with a simple computer program. You can also use the examples that I have given in this book to better understand how color can be a virtual mix of different colors. From the color dots, I have created a Sally Fretwell line of eco-friendly paint colors which you can order using contact information in the back of this book.

The Power of Color

How we see a color is directly related to what other contrasting or complementary colors shade, tone and surround it. A rainbow, created by colors separated by the prism of a million raindrops, illustrates the blending affect of a sequence of colors. We use color charts in a paint store, but unlike Nature, color charts group similar colors or similar shades of color. Contrast a paint chart, in your mind, with the picture of the brightly colored parrots from the Brazilian jungle that can naturally illustrate a teal color, next to reds, yellows and blues. Both "charts," one man made and one occurring naturally, have merit and can be used when deciding on a paint color. My goal is to show many examples of the subtle blending of colors such as in the natural shades of the flamingo as well as examples of contrasting but complementary colors such as those seen in a peacock, parrot or tropical fish.

This book has been created to give a series of visual stimuli that will enable you to think about what colors you like and why you like them. You may love the Caribbean photographs in this book but find those of Venice not very interesting at all. The colors exhibited by the Arizona canyon may make you want to investigate them further while the colors of autumn in Maine may elicit a "been there, done that" visual response. My aim is to help you discover what you like and dislike in a broad palette of colors.

The colors I pull out of the pictures are a few of the many that I personally can visualize "playing well together". Each is a stand alone color that I can see being used as a wall color or a combination of colors when decorating. You may say, "I love a color in the tropical fish" and want to use it with one of the Arizona canyon colors. This book is intended to serve as a visually stimulating guide that will entice you to enjoy and consider trying new colors. It will help you to identify what colors you like and in what combinations you can use them. The colors you see in the photographs play off of each other. From a design perspective, I find them very interesting. Sometimes colors

of a picture jump out and grab you, so that you can not help but notice them. In other instances, it is the subtle and barely discernible colors that work together to combine into a beautiful shade or tone to form a color that "pops"!

The picture of the Arizona canyon has both subtle and strong color variations that include lovely shades of pinks and oranges that have melded together after millions of years of paintwork done by the sun, sand, wind and water. The combined colors enhance and play off each other. They are complementary but when combined with other colors like blue or green, they would completely shift how you perceived the orange or pink color.

I love the shots of Venice and Italy. The buildings are sun and water faded versions of once stronger and more vibrant colors. Venice is a city known for its art and artists. With its faded but still colorful facades, accented by the clear blue sky and green-watered canals, Venice seems to be the work of a master artist who subtlety, but skillfully, muted and blended a vast array of colors into a masterpiece that creates a special feeling. These colors, combined with the unique architecture, created by centuries of different cultural and religious influences, give Venice it own unique feel that has been admired for years. The colorful boats, vibrant flowers in window boxes and bright awnings contrast and complement the faded stucco buildings. Adding water, with the fluid motion of the boats in the ever present canals, brings a different feel to the color than similar colors in the solidity of the Arizona canyons. The pictures that show Burano, an island off the coast of Italy, with the bright colored houses, stand in sharp contrast to the faded colors of Venice. Each color stands alone, but directly affects its neighboring colors, creating a vibrancy that is further enhanced by the bright, blue waters surrounding the town.

The colors of Venice, with its yellows, golds, salmons and reds provide a feeling which is quite different when compared to the yellows, golds, salmons and reds of an island paradise like Aruba. That is both the wonder and power of color. It can transcend and encompass. The seaside pictures of Aruba shout, "I want to go on vacation in a place like this, lie in the sun, sail in the clear blue waters and never come home," while the colors of Venice might provide a more subtle, reflective and soothingly warm feeling.

I chose the pictures of the cocktail drinks in Aruba because I love the stark, bold drink colors that have a transparency that is contained by the glass but with the backdrop of the uncontained

7

vastness of the sea. It easily illustrates how a bright green, an almost artificial color, works well with the natural aqua sea color. Beachy throw pillows and colorful flip flops combine with softer but strongly saturated colors like the variation in the orange rind/cherry garnish. These drinks, vibrantly colored, exude the joyous freedom of being on vacation in a tropical paradise with less inhibition and creating a mood all its own. Clients of mine that dare to use such vibrant colors mimic that feeling. They are less inhibited and do not feel bound by what might be considered a normal or safe color.

Color can create a mood. Color has the ability to transform, change, rejuvenate, invigorate, inspire and bring life. The key to picking colors, that have a special appeal, does not have to happen by pure guesswork. It does require learning to look below the surface, behind the colors, to discover what colors and color combinations work for you or what is the setting, the feeling or mood you are trying to achieve or duplicate.

What is it that makes the color or combination of colors work? Why does a color feel good? I am sure that there is a psychological reason for why we feel a certain bonding with certain colors. I am inclined to offer a simple approach to color and the attraction we feel for certain ones. It might be that you grew up in a bedroom that was painted with a similar color or maybe you love the panorama of colors associated with springtime flowers. It might be the dark green stems and leaves blooming into colorful petals of pinks, reds, yellows, or golds that meld together to create striking combinations, naturally created and indelibly imprinted on our minds. This natural vibrancy of flowers with a blue sky background not only creates a visual imprint but also evokes other physical feelings such as the warmth of the sun, the sweet scent of the flowers or a warm breeze caressing your face. Colors and other senses combine to create a certain mood, a unique feeling related to the color or colors. They make an impression that we enjoying recreating time and time again, even when the blooms have long past faded.

Purple Haze

Perpetual Pink

Forever Green

Aruba Sun

Aruba Burst

Aruba Sea

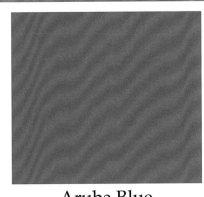

Aruba Blue

When you look at any picture, you are consciously and subconsciously affected by the color. When you view a beach scene, a multitude of responses and memories may come to mind: the warm water of the ocean, salt air, fluidity, ever present movement, sandcastles, crabs, dolphins, whales, summer, time off, no work, being outdoors, less clothes, suntanned skin, fresh air, walking in the sand, sunshine, tropical drinks with funny umbrellas, sensuous nights, succulent fresh fish and shrimp dinners, cookouts, family vacations, bright beach umbrellas and beach chairs, wicker furniture, honeymoons, hunting for sea shells, starry nights, the sound of crashing waves and the list can go on and on.

When you leave the beach, you can not completely recreate all these sense related delights. You can recreate the colors from a memory, though, and in doing so, you pull in all the other sensual memories to create a special wall color that enables you to conjure up all the delights of past beach visits.

Once a person understands color from a warm/cold perspective and takes into consideration the peripheral context of color, they will understand how to make colors play well together. In trying to recreate the color of the ocean, it is not just the ocean that has to be copied but it is also the hypnotic comfort of the sound of lapping waves and the warmth of the sun and sand. All are relaxing, inviting and a part of the overall color. So an azure color with a lot of warmth added to it, next to an appropriately placed colorful picture or fabric, may very well create a different feeling than if it is with navy blue and gray tones. You may have a beautiful aqua couch made with a fabric that will "pop" when you put it together with colors that draw out the warmth in the aqua coloring. A single color may have many different variations of tone, feel and warmth depending on what other colors you surround it with.

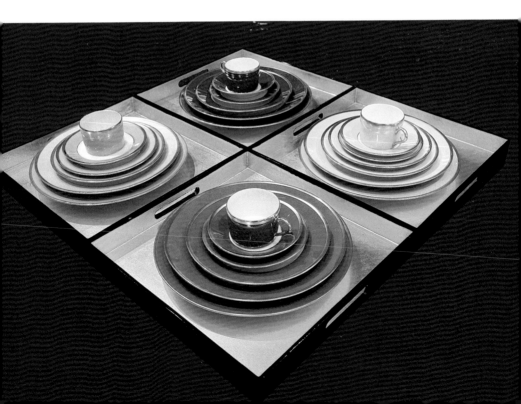

Luminous Beige

Clay Baked

Peaceful Green

Duck Bill

Purple Duck

Duck Pond

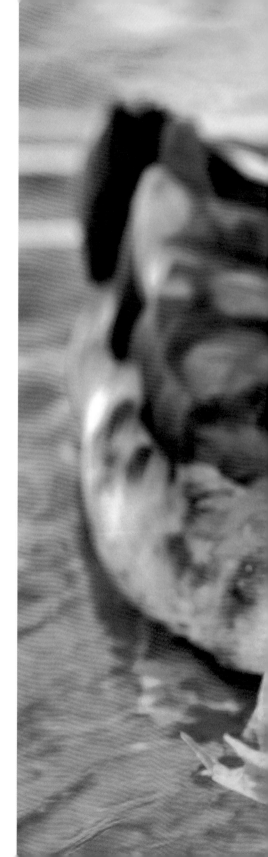

Mandarin Teal

Mandarin Sand

Mandarin Wheat

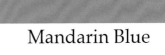

Mandarin Blue

Closely related to how the eye perceives color is how the mind subconsciously interprets color. When you look at a picture, place or thing, your eye will focus on the color but the mind will subconsciously add elements to your perception of that color. It will tell you if it is a color that you recognize as having seen before, where you have seen it and what memories that are associated with that color. Thusly, if you have a favorite color

which brings forth positive memories and you paint a room with that color, each time you enter that room, your eye will focus on that color in your field of vision and subconsciously your mind will instinctively bring forth the reasons for your love of that color. This will add to the overall understanding and positive reaction to that particular color.

I love color and enjoy having someone say to me, "Wow, I now love the kitchen and the color I painted it". In most cases though, before a client reaches the point where they will try a new color, they will usually say, "I am afraid to try that color and want to stick with something that is safe even though I am not sure I really like it." I often have to push clients to experiment, to take a chance, to try something new in order to find out if they like a color and if it will work for them. I recognize and understand the concerns of my clients but at the same time I want them to delve a little deeper, to push the envelope and try colors they would not normally consider using. Given the chance, I know it will be a color that they will end up falling in love with.

Sunny Side

Terrace Green

Faded Stucco

The rich, warm colors of the Southwest, with its salmon, mustard, gold, pink, browns, red and orange tones, mixed with different textures, open blue sky and abundant sunlight exude a richness, depth and vast openness that define the region. These tones are the warmest of paint colors. They draw in the light and have a calming effect. Inhabitants of this part of the United States love these colors because of the way this part of the country makes them feel. This feeling is a direct result of the colors that surround them in nature. When used in doctor's offices or restaurants, these color schemes create a decompressing effect on all those that enter and helping them to relax.

There are colors that grab your attention. It might be a color in a picture, advertisement, building façade, piece of clothing or artwork. It could occur naturally as in a sunrise, sunset or autumn landscape. Many people see colors that they like but have trouble translating that color onto a bathroom wall, kitchen interior or a swatch of fabric for a living room settee. We all see colors that stand out in our memory or a color that works or creates a nice feeling. Having the confidence to translate that color feeling into "I could paint my kitchen in that tone" is a skill that I hope this book will help you develop.

Venitian Straw

Terra Cotta Pot

Venitian Skiff Blue

In humans, there are higher concentrations of color-sensitive cone cells in the central region of the retina. As a result, when you look at a panoramic view of nature, your eye will naturally focus on the color of the center of your visual field. However, subconsciously, that focal color is also affected by what is on the periphery. Since it is on the periphery and not the focal point, then your mind adds it to the equation or totality of the overall picture.

Frank Lloyd Wright once said, "Study nature, love nature, stay close to nature. It will never fail you." These words, relating to architecture, ring absolutely true when used in choosing colors. We might not all have the chance to travel to the extremes of the northern hemisphere to view the beautiful colors created by the aurora borealis but we do not have to travel much further than outside our front door to experience the many examples of color that Nature has to offer. Who does not feel better or cheered up when seeing beautiful samples of color in your back yard, a park, mountain, desert or seashore? The task, though, is to be able to pull the colors inside and to surround yourself with that natural warmth of feeling. The next time you go for a walk, take the time to notice the colors along your path. Take the time not only to explore the vast array of colors that you encounter but also to visually isolate a certain color that you like. Notice not only how that color stands alone but also how it combines with surrounding colors.

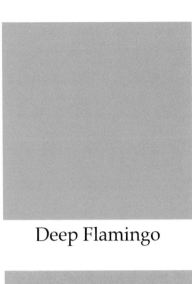

Deep Flamingo

Warm Glow

Flamingo Wing

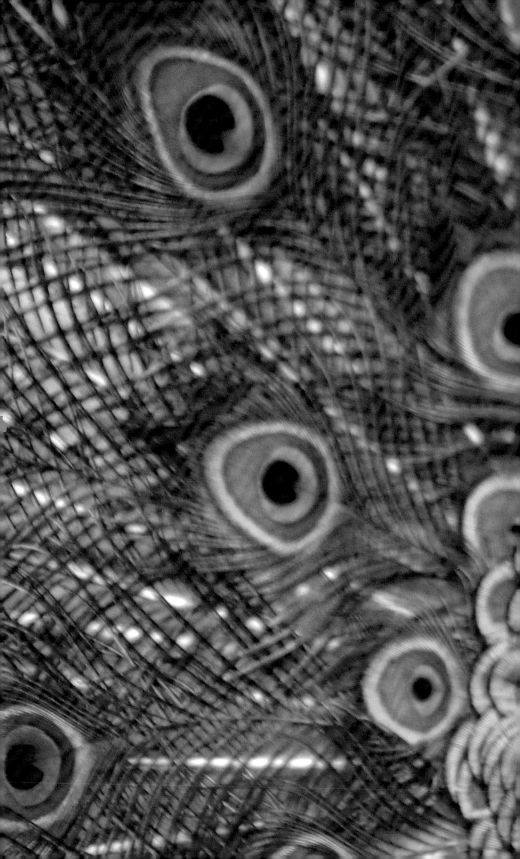

Cocktail Lemon

Oasis Green

Party Sky

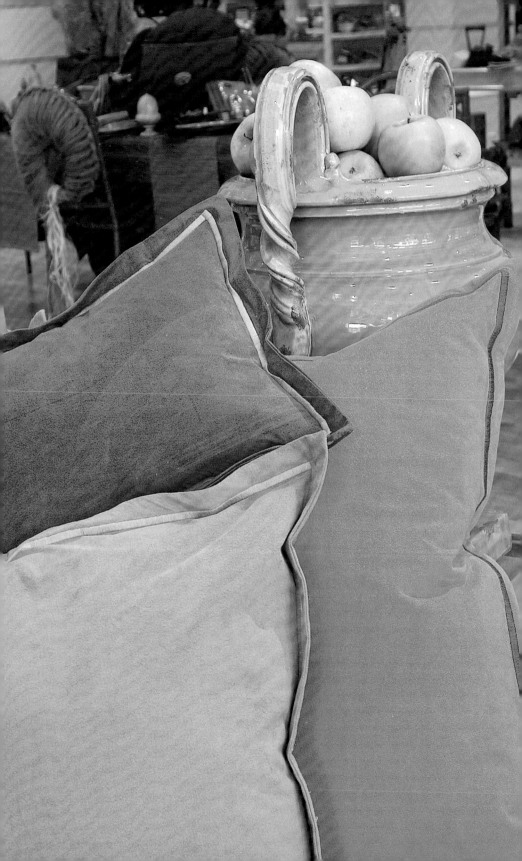

Many times, when remodeling, someone will change the wall color and then everything visually surrounding that color changes in relationship to the new color. They create not only a different colored room but a room with a different feel. For example, a gray tile with gray walls will feel one way. The same gray tile with walls painted a warmer color, like salmon or gold, would feel completely different. The warmer colors in the tile are drawn out by the warm colors of the wall. The key to picking tile, fabric or wall colors has to come first from understanding what you are trying to achieve. If you are duplicating nature or a place that you love to visit, such as a favorite restaurant, a friend's house or a location you have vacationed such as the Southwest or the shore, then try to visualize and transpose that favorite color onto the room where you want that color duplicated.

Raving Orange

Exploding Yellow

Rosey Morning

Is a red a yellow-gold red or a blue-red? One feels warm with the one and austere with the other. Color chips in the paint store can be deceiving. The chip, more often than not, is surrounded by similar colors which can distort the color in your mind's eye. By itself, the paint chip is not the same color you are going to see on your wall, if painted that color. The color on the wall is the bottom line. When painting do not hesitate to experiment

and buy a smaller amount of paint and coat a small portion of the area you want to paint. In this way, you can get a more exact feel of how that paint will look. Do not be discouraged if you like a color and it looks horrible on a wall. Do no give up! Try a warmer tone of the same color. Many times we will choose a color we think is what we want but it may turn out to be too stark or cold and we may have to try other tones to get it right.

I have found through years of practical trial and experimentation that it is important, when choosing a color, to consider whether it will be highlighted by natural light or man-made light. Also important is whether or not the color will be combined with natural or man-made tones. These differences can completely alter what a color may look like and the mood that the color will create. Warm rich tones, such as a red in a kitchen combined with light, off-white cabinets, will feel different than the same red when combined with dark, wood cabinets. You may love that red with the off-white cabinets and find it falls dead with the darker wood cabinets. This is an easy example that illustrates that color is very much affected by its surroundings in a multitude of ways. A painted wall will also be affected by how it is lit. Lighting will greatly determine how a color is perceived. If it receives a lot of natural sunlight it will look different at different times of the day.

Why do the Sedona Mountains (see following page) feel so grounding and warm? The vast sky, blue-green color, the warmth of the sun, the texture of the clay type rocks, the mineral gold's, coppers and terra-cottas are very relaxing and the combination of the elements are cheery, uplifting and inviting.

Firey Maple

New England Linger

Fabulous Fall

Filo Dough

Bread Crust

Red Sunflower

1. Look to see what it is that you like about a color or that you would like to duplicate and consider where you have seen it before.

2. Why is it you like that color? Most often you will find that it is associated with a setting you love, a color you "discovered" on a vacation, a favorite place in the outdoors or a warm, comforting color from your childhood.

3. What colors in the room you are painting or decorating would you like to draw out or accentuate? Perhaps you would like to bring out the warm, natural and earthy tones of a wood floor or the woodwork of your kitchen cabinets?

4. Perhaps you want to use a color that will naturally draw in sunlight from the outdoors. How much light do you naturally have? If you are redoing a whole room or even choosing colors for a newly built house, try to bring an order and sense of what the color palettes would be used together and what you want the total, overall effect to be.

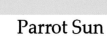

Parrot Sun

Parrot Blue

Crown Royale

Parrot Teal

Trigger Home

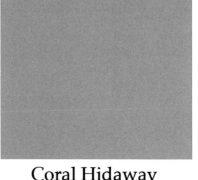

Coral Hidaway

Trigger Lips

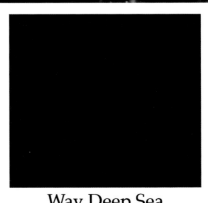

Way Deep Sea

We know from basic art class that there are three primary colors: red, blue and yellow. All other colors, the different shades, tones and variations are based on those three major colors. Just as we know that there is a red, we also know that there can be a lollipop red, an Irish setter red, a firecracker red, a fire in the fireplace red, a sunburn red, a sunset red, a Santa Claus red, an apple red, a wine red, a stop light red, a cardinal red, a cherry red and the inside of a ripe watermelon red.

The identification of color relates to our sense of vision but, in truth, our mind's determination of color is based on so much more. A color we view, whether it is a primary color or the multitudes of variations created by combining red, blue and yellow, is strongly influenced by our memory of color, like a taste we associate with a certain food we love. Reds, yellows and autumn browns can evoke the feeling of jumping into a pile of fallen leaves on a cool autumn day. Color has the power to conjure up in our minds more than just the significance of a color.

Palm Green

Sea Kyak Pink

Tranquil Sea

21

Tulip Tips   Totally Tulip

Toulouse LauTulip

Tulip Passion

Flower Power Pink

Parisian Yellow

Passion Orange

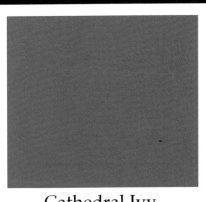

Cathedral Ivy

Have you ever read an article by a food critic where they talk about the "presentation" of the food? The food critic views the sum of the parts and rates the whole of the dining experience. The food critic not only tastes the food, but looks at the color of the food, how it is arranged on the plate when it is served, how appetizing it looks and smells and how one type of food tastes in combination with other foods that are served with it, in short, how it is "presented." In the same way, the color, lighting, textures, accent pieces, pillows, pictures, furniture, floor color and window treatments all combine to create the whole.

Daybreak Pink

Sunset Pink

Meadow Green

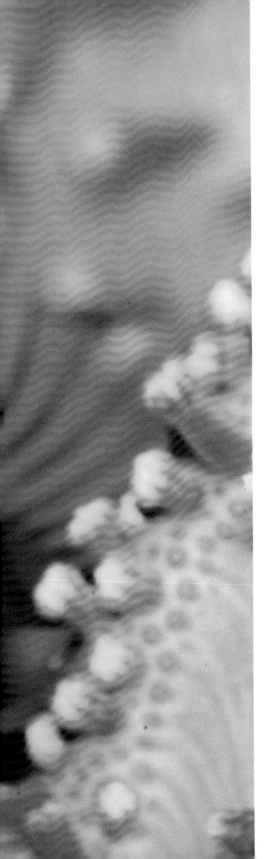

So am I suggesting you chose a blue fish color for a room in your home? Not at all, but I just love this picture of a tropical fish surrounded by beautifully colored sea life. Maybe it is the big, inquisitive eyes and surprised smile on its' face or the warm memories of a line from the Dr. Seuss poem, "One fish, two fish, red fish, blue fish...," that I used to read to my children or the exotic appeal of sea life that I might see when snorkeling on a Caribbean reef but this picture tugs at my heart. I am a firm believer that if a color brings warmth to your soul and a smile to your face then you should find a way to bring it into your life.

Sedona Canyon

Sedona Clay

Sedona Terrace

Party Pink

Cocktail Green

Caribbean Teal

Each and every day, Nature offers a cornucopia of colors which we can bring into our lives. All you have to do is open your eyes the next time you walk out the door, visit the seashore, take a drive in the country or view the Discovery Channel. There are sunsets and sunrises, rainbows and bolts of lightening framed by storm clouds during a summer storm. There are rays of sunlight dancing on the water as a school of dolphins breaks through the surface on a brief, but glorious, airborne flight. There is the sun suddenly beaming down on you as it peaks from behind the clouds on a cloudy day, changing the whole landscape of color before you in the blink of an eye. There is the burst of greens and blues you experience when you watch a peacock open and display its feathered treasure chest of color or the hues and richness of a freshly baled field of hay, with ripples of heat distorting the idyllic landscape. There is the richness of the Sedona Mountains with its plethora of vibrant earth tones. The panoramic view of a multitude of colored fish species, swimming amongst a vast backdrop of multi-colored coral. Every day, everywhere, every moment there is color to be seen, observed, enjoyed and explored. To recreate it, to bring it into your home or living and working space is the key to creating a living space that will enliven and rejuvenate your life.

Burano Canal

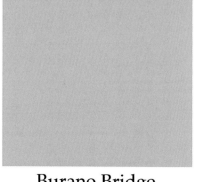

Burano Bridge

Burano Clay

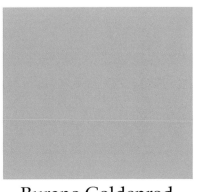

Burano Goldenrod

Venitian Butter

Venitian Pasta

Venitian Wine

Venitian Bagette

I have always loved the color combinations that Caspari puts together as evidenced by the picture above. You can walk into a Caspari store and immediately be assured of a stimulating color experience. You can learn from their knowledgeable staff, who will actively engage you, in a user-friendly way, into the world of their color. They have years of expertise in this area, which they are more than happy to share with you. You will leave their store knowing you have what you want and the confidence to bring it into your own home.

Ultimately every room in your home can be a space that you can enjoy being in. Color can lead you to that enjoyment. Whether your goal is to have an inviting and vibrant kitchen to cook and entertain in or a cozy bedroom where you curl up and read at night, color can make all the difference in attaining that goal.

Color and the effective use of color go well beyond just improving the feel in a home. I have seen doctor's offices and medical facilities transformed through the use of inviting colors, from a space where patients who enter suffer from "white coat syndrome," to a place where patients actually feel relaxed and comforted and do not mind returning.

Businesses, restaurants, malls and offices that I have consulted have all said that altering their use of color has completely changed how both employees and customers feel about their surroundings. They report that sales, production and the over-all work environment have greatly benefited from the color changes that were made.

Color has that kind of power. From the workplace to the home, color has both physical and psychological effects on us. It can make you feel better emotionally, become more uplifted, less tired, more relaxed, and in general affect your over-all well-being.

All of these things achieved by a simple coat of paint... that's the power of color.

Photo Copyrights

Courtesy of Caspari, Inc, Charlottesville, VA: 20, 21, 42, 114
Dan Addison: 4, 14, 54, 86, 106
Eric Roth: 39
Eric Roth Photography, Susan Sargent designer: Cover, 12, 60, 67, 75, 90
John C G Thompson: Cover, 6, 20, 21, 32, 42, 44, 56, 58, 96, 112, 114
Philip Beaurline: 40
Scott Taylor: Cover, 26, 30, 34, 84
TAL Y BONT: 99
www.iStockPhoto.com/Anglocentricity: 88
"/aradan: 9
"/Brytta: 46
"/CapturedNuance: 5, 72
"/Chiclac: 92
"/DanSchmitt: 82
"/DarrenGreen: 36, 104
"/dhare: 102
"/Enjoylife2: 18
"/Fabphoto: 80
"/Giacomo: 22
"/Hannahgleg: 109
"/illureh: 1
"/Izanoza: 24
"/Khine: 62
"/Killroy: 100
"/Lisay: 10
"/Marcviln: 76
"/MarkLee: 70
"/Marlee90: 98
"/Mjutabor: 28
"/naturesdisplay: Cover, 57
"/Rainlady: Cover, 52
"/rricozzi: 50
"/saraphic06: 78
"/Saturated: 110
"/ShawnWaite: 49
"/shooterguy: 16
"/SurpassPro: 68
"/tiplea84: 48
"/tommyleong: 64

Sally Fretwell

Sally Fretwell is certified by the American Society of Interior Designers to teach her continuing education classes and is also available for consultation. For more information on her classes, consultation and other books call, email or write her at:

Sally Fretwell

1-888- 830-1860

sally@sallyfretwell.com

www.sallyfretwell.com

You may order the Sally Fretwell paint colors by email. An order form and information on the paints and paint chips seen in this book are posted on the website. There are 70 beautiful colors to choose from and each one has a name referenced in the book. Do not hesitate to contact Sally if you have any questions.